MOMENTS *in* LIFE
by
CLAUDINE

MOMENTS *in* LIFE
by
CLAUDINE

Claudine Frye

Pentland Press, Inc.
www.pentlandpressusa.com

PUBLISHED BY PENTLAND PRESS, INC.
5122 Bur Oak Circle, Raleigh, North Carolina 27612
United States of America
919-782-0281

ISBN 1-57197-283-8
Library of Congress Control Number: 2001 130319

Copyright © 2001 Claudine Frye
All rights reserved, which includes the right to reproduce
this book or portions thereof in any form whatsoever
except as provided by the U.S. Copyright Law.

Printed in the United States of America

Moment of Dedication

To my twin sister, my friend, my confidant:

We've been together since the womb and it has been a joy! We have laughed and cried with one another when there was no one else. Thank you for loving me unconditionally and always being there for me. *Moments in Life by Claudine* would not be in print without your continued support. Thanks for allowing me to give others a brief look at "moments" in your life through some of my poetry. I pray that God will grant you only good "moments" and that you will embrace them. If you are confronted with bad "moments," I trust you will see them as simply challenges to conquer. You are a wonderful mother, a great wife, a God-loving woman and the best sister. I was sharing a problem we were having while mother was ill with a woman who does not have a sister and she said, "If that is what it is like to have a sister, I am glad I don't have one." I thought to myself, *What does a disagreement have to do with love for one's sister?* She obviously did not have a clue about unconditional love. I respect you and I am not sure how I would survive without you. I have learned so much from you. This twin thing has been and continues to be a great "moment!"

I love you Clot.

Moment of Thanks

GOD:
　　Thank you for being a part of my life. For choosing me as the vehicle to write *Moments in Life by Claudine*. I know it comes from you because I get comfort from reading or hearing my poetry read.

MOTHER:
　　Thanks for giving me your name, Claudine. I loved being called "little Claudine" growing up. I am thankful for your strength, I have it! You had some very sad moments in your life, mother. However, through all the abuse, you were the strongest woman I have ever known. I wish you had known how beautiful and what a loving woman you really were. I know you knew your children loved you. With every opportunity, we tried to protect you. I now realize that your happiness was your job! I love you mother and miss you dearly. Thank you for teaching me how to love unconditionally. I know you are saying to the angels, "My daughter is something else, isn't she?"

JACLYN CLAUDINE:
　　Hey STINK. I bet you wish I would not call you that for you are now 21 years old. But we both know at this point in life, it has nothing to do with an odor. I love you as if I gave birth to you. I am so very proud of you Jaclyn. I know it has not been easy for you with the absence of your father in your life. Your mother and I have tried

to protect you from the life-altering affects for a young girl who does not have nurturing from her daddy. Because we know the damage it can cause. In spite of some not-so-good moments in your life, you have blossomed into a very beautiful and strong woman. Thank you for allowing me to learn from the sharing of your moments with me. And thanks for letting me share my moments with you. Your Aunt Claudine, your second mommy, loves you very much!

JEWISH FAMILY SERVICES, PROJECT CHAI:
To Brynna, Kathy, and Jill. When I could not find help anywhere, I found JFS, Project Chai. You helped me save my soul and possibly my life. The hole I speak of in my poetry was real and you helped me climb my way back to reality. Brynna, the first day of our session on overcoming powerlessness, I remember you saying, "It's not about your husbands, boyfriends, mothers, fathers, etc. It is about YOU!" I thought to myself, *I will not be back. She does not have a clue. Wasn't she listening? We all have either been abused verbally, emotionally, financially, physically or psychologically by someone.* Well, the rest is history. Thank God I had the good sense to return to the sessions. Kathy, I know you are missed at JFS. I feel very emotional when I think of where I was when I first met you and how far I have come. Thank you for re-enforcing to me that no one provokes anyone to abuse. Abuse is a choice. If only you could see me now! And Jill. You came in near the end of this life-changing moment but are nonetheless important. Your continued belief in me and support will always be a factor in my emotional wellness. Thanks to JFS, I have overcome powerlessness!

REV. CHRIS:
You are a true woman of God and my dear friend. Living in a city without family was difficult during the tough moments in my life but you helped to fill that void. I thank God for sending you to me. I remember the first day you walked into church. I knew we would be close. You have always been there for me. Most of all, I thank you for loving my family and the courage to get involved.

MALVA:
What can I say to you? You have always been so supportive of my continued need to grow spiritually and emotionally. I will always treasure your unconditional love and friendship. Thanks for many memorable moments.

ZAKIA:
You have taught me more about endurance than almost anyone. Thanks for allowing me to be godmother to Jamila and Sarai in your absence. Thank you for a friendship I know comes from the heart. You have been in Morocco for the past five years, but that has not diminished the depth of our mutual love and respect for one another. I have watched the girls say their prayers many times and I wrote, "I Wish My Mommy Was Here." I pray that you will continue to fight to be with your children. They love and need you. Thank you Zakia and may God grant you your heart's desire to be reunited with your daughters.

JAMILA AND SARAI:
I realize you are too young, ages five and six, to understand the impact you have had on Aunt Claudine's life. Thank you for allowing me to keep your mommy alive in your hearts and minds. I know how much you want and need her to come home. Thank you for giving me a real glimpse of motherhood. But always remember, no one can take the place of mommy. I love you both!

SONYA:
Thank you for loving me. You are sixteen now but I remember, when you were very young, feeling loved by you. I will treasure our moments of discussion. We would form a circle, you, Sylvia, Cordel, Justin, and me, and just talk about everything. You guys were very young but boy did I learn a lot from you all. Thank you for sharing my publishing success with your class at Beaumont School. Thank you for your prayers. You may be young but I know you are a child of God. God bless you, sweetheart.

BRENDA BROWN, LILLIAN BRANDYBURG, DIANNE DOBROVIC and LYDIA MEYER:

To my sisters in friendship. Thank you all for believing in me and loving me. "Girlfriend" was written because of moments I have spent with each of you. I have gained an abundance of treasures, not materially speaking, that will be comfort to me always. Thank you for teaching me many things about myself. Unconditional love is hard to find in girlfriends. I am blessed because I know I have it with you all. Hey Girlfriends!

Contents

FOREWORD	xiii
THE PITTER PATTER OF LITTLE FEET	1
DADDY, WHY?	2
THAT HURTS ME	4
SLEEPLESS NIGHTS	7
LOVE ME GENTLY	9
IT'S BEEN FIVE YEARS	10
WE CALLED HIM GILLIGAN	12
I DO	14
GIRL, SAY IT AIN'T SO	16
GIRLFRIEND	19
THE DANCE	21
HE LOVES ME, HE LOVES ME NOT	23
OPPOSITES	25
WE JUST DON'T ANYMORE	27
YOUR SCENT	29
THE "N" WORD	30
THE WEDDING BAND	33
ESPECIALLY ON MOTHER'S DAY	35
HAPPY BIRTHDAY, CLOT	37
I WISH MY MOMMY WAS HERE	41
HOMELESS	43
FOREVER CAME EARLY	45

I'M OUT OF HERE	47
ON NIGHTS LIKE THIS	49
STAY IN CONTROL	51
MY CHILD THAT NEVER WAS	53
THAT UNRELENTING STARE	55
THIS PAIN THIS HEARTACHE	57
LET'S SNEAK AWAY	59
YOUR WORDS	61
LOST POWER	62
WILL YOU BE MINE?	64
THE STRANGER IN MY BED	67
I MISSED YOU TODAY	69
HANDCUFFED	70
MY MIND IS WAITING FOR MY HEART	73
I DIDN'T GET TO SAY GOODBYE	75
THE DAMAGE RUNS TOO DEEP	77
ON MY OWN	79

Foreword

By Claudia Mitchell – Author's Twin Sister

We have always been close partly because we are family but mostly because our moments began from conception. We have laughed and cried together, worked and played together and have made many memories that no one else will ever share.

We didn't always have a lot but we always knew we had each other. You are my twin sister, the one I can call any time day or night, and I know you will be there for me.

I don't think I have been more proud of you than I am now. It fills my heart with joy witnessing your tremendous success in publishing your first book of poetry. You see, I did say first book because there is so much love and compassion within you I know there will be many books to come.

I have watched you grow through much pain from relationship issues, infertility, and the loss of our dear mother. And yet, you have renewed your spirit and have risen above it all with much pride and peace in your life.

Sharing one's life moments, good and bad, with the world shows a tremendous amount of courage and I salute you.

What I have enjoyed most are the moments that you, Greg, John and I have shared. There would always be a moment when I would say, "Claudine read us something," and of course you would. Then there were the moments when you were so wonderfully funny that John or I would say to Greg, "She needs to take that act on the road."

You always had dreams of being a mother. I remember the two of us spending many moments as teens talking about growing up and having children. It never happened for you. We now know that God had a special plan in store for you.

I have watched you be a mother to many disenfranchised children, your goddaughters, and especially to my daughter Jaclyn. Like our husbands, Jaclyn learned at a very early age that you and I come as a packaged deal. (smile)

Thank you for all the times you have been there for Jaclyn when I could not. You are a wonderful, compassionate, funny and caring wife. Whenever you tell me about the "red light specials" you put together for Greg, I envy your creativity.

We are all blessed to have shared special moments with you. And with God's grace, we will be blessed with many, many more. We have both changed a lot through the years and so have things around us. The one thing that has not changed is the special bond between us that keeps us close to one another no matter where we are.

Even more precious to me than all we shared when we were young is the love and closeness we share today. You are my dear and loving sister and my very special friend.

I love you,
Clot

THE PITTER PATTER OF LITTLE FEET

WE FINALLY GET THEM ALL TUCKED IN
PRAYERS SAID BOOKS READ FROM BEGINNING TO END
KISSES GIVEN AND WITHOUT A DOUBT
THEY'RE ASLEEP WE TIP TOE OUT

WE POUR A GLASS OF SOMETHING COOL
GETTING CLOSE LIKE IN HIGH SCHOOL
ALONE AT LAST WHAT A TREAT
AND THEN THE PITTER PATTER OF LITTLE FEET

I'M SCARED THERE'S A MONSTER IN MY ROOM
DADDY CHASE HIM OUT GET THE BROOM
OFF TO BED AGAIN WE GO
MOM DAD THE KIDS IN TOW

HONEY, WAKE UP I THINK IT'S LATE
SO MUCH FOR OUR LAST NIGHT'S DATE
WE STUMBLE PASS THE COOL DRINK
THAT NOW IS WARM
FALL INTO BED IN EACH OTHER'S ARMS

WE WANT TO SLEEP IN WE'RE TIRED WE'RE BEAT
BUT HERE COMES THE PITTER PATTER OF LITTLE FEET

CRAWLING INTO OUR BED ASKING, "ARE YOU STILL 'SLEEP?"
WE TRY TO PRETEND BUT THEY DON'T MISS A BEAT
AN ELBOW HERE A KNEE THERE
WITHOUT THE ASKING OUR BED WE SHARE
"I'M HUNGRY I WANT TO EAT"
OUT OF BED DOWN THE HALL
PITTER PATTER LITTLE FEET

WHEN YOU TRY TO PLAN A DATE TOGETHER
TAKE THE KIDS THAT YOU SO TREASURE
TO GRANDMA'S OR ACROSS THE STREET
OR HEAR THE PITTER PATTER OF LITTLE FEET

DADDY, WHY?

MOM IS PUSHING FOR ME TO UNCURL
HONEY IT'S TIME TO ENTER THE WORLD
ANOTHER PUSH AND I'M OUT WITH A CRY
YOU'RE NOT HERE DADDY, WHY?

MUMPS, MEASLES, WHOOPING COUGH TOO
MOMMY DID HER BEST TO MAKE IT THROUGH
IN THE MIDDLE OF THE NIGHT WHEN I WOULD CRY
ONLY MOMMY WOULD COME DADDY, WHY?

I'M A KID I WANT IT ALL
JUMP ROPE SOCCER AND BASEBALL
WITH CLOTHES SHOES AND SCHOOL SUPPLIES
SO MUCH I MISSED DADDY, WHY?

I'M GRADUATING FROM HIGH SCHOOL
LATER TODAY
ONE LAST STEP AND I'M ON MY WAY
I GRADUATE WITH HONORS
AND MOM'S ON HIGH
YOU'RE NOT HERE DADDY, WHY?

WALKING THROUGH THAT COLLEGE DOOR
THE BOOKS THE CLASSES WHAT A CHORE
I GET BY EXCEPT FOR ONE THING
I'VE NEVER BEEN GOOD WITH THE DATING SCENE

LOW SELF ESTEEM AND NOT QUITE SURE
OF WHO I AM AND WHAT LOVE IS FOR
EMOTIONALLY I'M JUST GETTING BY
TELL ME DADDY, WHY?

NO ONE CAN FILL THIS EMPTY SPACE
IT'S FOR MY DADDY JUST IN CASE

MARRIAGES KIDS I'VE DONE IT ALL
SOME WOULD SAY I'VE NOT MISSED A CALL
I SMILE AND SIMPLY SAY WITH A SIGH
LIFE'S BEEN OKAY DADDY, WHY?

THAT HURTS ME

PLEASE DON'T YELL, THAT SCARES ME
WHY CAN'T WE JUST LET IT GO?
AT TIMES YOU'RE SOMEONE I HARDLY KNOW
PLEASE JUST LET IT BE
THAT HURTS ME

MY TEARS ARE REAL
THE PAIN I TRY TO CONCEAL
I'M BRUISED INSIDE AND OUT
BELIEVE ME WITHOUT A DOUBT
THAT HURTS ME

MY DAD DID IT
MY UNCLES DID IT
MY NEIGHBORS DID IT
AND MY MOM WOULD FLEE
IT STILL HURTS ME

YOUR ARMS ENGULF ME
COMFORTING MY SOUL
IN JUST A MOMENT
YOUR EMBRACE IS COLD
YOUR SILENCE REVEALS SO VERY MUCH
WHAT HAPPENED TO THAT GENTLE TOUCH?
YOUR DISTANCE IS A MYSTERY
THAT HURTS ME

THE PUSH THE SHOVE
THE THREATS MAKE NO SENSE
A SIMPLE QUESTION AND SOON YOU'RE TENSE
WHO HAS THE HEALING REMEDY?
THAT HURTS ME

MY CRY FOR HELP IS SHADOWED BY MY SMILE
I WORK I PLAY IN PAIN ALL THE WHILE
A PROMISE A GIFT A KISS TO MAKE THINGS BETTER
A BAND-AID FIX FOR SOMETHING GREATER

A WISH FOR YOU TO HEAL MY PAIN
WHEN ALL ALONG YOUR PAIN'S THE SAME
IT'S HARDLY POSSIBLE TO SOOTHE MY SOUL
WHEN CRAWLING FROM YOUR OWN DEEP HOLE

SLEEPLESS NIGHTS

THE TICK TOCK OF THE CLOCK
THE LIGHTED NUMBERS GLARING
I THINK IT'S BEEN HOURS
AT THE CEILING I'M STILL STARING

TEAR DROPS OF MOISTURE
SLIDE DOWN MY FACE
SHOWERING MY SOUL
AT A CREEPING PACE

A HEAVY HEART AND A SAD SPIRIT
DAWN WILL COME AND OH HOW I CHEER IT

SLEEPLESS NIGHTS MORNINGS FILLED WITH GLOOM
MAYBE JUST MAYBE I'LL FEEL BETTER
BY NOON

LOVE ME GENTLY

SLOWLY SLIDE YOUR HANDS DOWN MY SPINE
MASSAGING MY THOUGHTS AND CARESSING MY MIND
I KNOW YOU WERE SENT HERE JUST FOR ME
I KNOW YOU'LL ALWAYS LOVE ME GENTLY

BRING YOUR BODY IN CLOSE TO MINE
ALLOW OUR DAY TO QUICKLY UNWIND
UNDRESS MY LONELINESS
AND CLOTHE MY SOUL
WHISPER YOU LOVE ME
FROM HEAD TO TOE

COVER MY FEARS WITH YOUR
BLANKET OF STRENGTH
ACKNOWLEDGE MY NEEDS WITH
A WELCOME INTEREST

I FEEL YOUR BREATH AS IT DANCES
ACROSS MY CHEST
DELIGHTING MY SENSES
DOING WHAT YOU DO BEST

YOUR SMELL OF WARMTH
FLOWS THROUGH THE AIR
PULL ME CLOSER TAKE US THERE

THE WORLD DISAPPEARS
IT'S YOU AND ME
FOREVER AND ALWAYS
LOVE ME GENTLY

IT'S BEEN FIVE YEARS

MOTHER IT'S BEEN FIVE YEARS

OUR HEARTS STILL ACHE
THE TEARS STILL FLOW
IT SEEMS LIKE YESTERDAY THAT
YOU HAD TO GO

YOUR VOICE WE DON'T HEAR
THE REASON YOU LEFT
HAS NEVER BEEN QUITE CLEAR

WE MISS YOU SO MUCH
YOU HAD A WAY
WITH YOUR GENTLE TOUCH

THE HOLIDAYS WERE SPECIAL FOR US ALL
THANKSGIVING CHRISTMAS
WE'D HAVE A BALL
THE GIFTS THE FOOD SPREADING GOOD CHEER
MOTHER HOW MUCH WE WISH YOU WERE HERE

IT'S BEEN FIVE YEARS

YOUR FACE WE SEE ONLY IN OUR DREAMS
BUT YOUR LOVING SPIRIT
IS ALWAYS AROUND IT SEEMS

REMEMBERING THE TIMES
WE LAUGHED 'TIL WE CRIED
WHAT FUN WE HAD WITH YOU BY OUR SIDE

NO ONE IN THE WORLD
COULD HAVE BEEN A BETTER MOTHER
IF WE HAD DONE THE CHOOSING
WE WOULD HAVE CHOSEN NO OTHER

PLEASE REST IN PEACE
WE KNOW YOUR MIND IS AT EASE
NO PAIN NO SUFFERING
JUST HEAVEN'S GENTLE BREEZE

WE CALLED HIM GILLIGAN

A PUFF OF WHITE FUR
THE COLOR OF SNOW
FOR SEVEN YEARS WE SMILED
WATCHING HIM GROW

GET THE BALL GET THE BALL
WE WOULD SAY
HE'D SEARCH AND SEARCH
WITH A LOOK OF DISMAY

FINALLY FOUND AND ROLLING BETWEEN HIS FEET
SOMEONE OH SOMEONE
PLAY SOCCER WITH ME

WE CALLED HIM GILLIGAN

HIS FAVORITE GAME WAS HIDE AND SEEK
HE'D BEG TO PLAY IT WEEK AFTER WEEK
IN THE CLOSET BEHIND THE DOOR YOU SILLY DOG
WANDERING AROUND LOST IN A FOG

AH GOTCHA HIS FACE WOULD SAY
AS HE RAN AND JUMPED IN VICTORY
IN HIS OWN WAY

WE CALLED HIM GILLIGAN

OUT FOR HIS WALK DOWN MEMORY LANE
POTTY POTTY GIL IT'S ABOUT TO RAIN
WHAT? CARRY YOU BACK?
HAVE YOU LOST YOUR MIND?
HIS LOOK WOULD SAY MOMMY DOES IT
ALL THE TIME

THE SWEATER OFF THE PAWS ARE DRIED
HE EXPECTS A TREAT FOR WHAT HE DID OUTSIDE

WE CALLED HIM GILLIGAN

GET IN YOUR BED GIL WE'LL BE RIGHT BACK
OBEDIENT ALWAYS THE COST A SNACK

OUT THE WINDOW HE'D GLARE
WHETHER MINUTES OR HOURS
WE CAN'T LOOK BACK
THAT FACE WHAT POWER

I HEAR A CAR THE GARAGE DOOR GOES UP
THEY'RE HOME HE BEAMS
WITH LICKING AND KISSING
FROM OUR DEAR PUP

WE CALLED HIM GILLIGAN

HE'S GOTTEN INTO THE TRASH AGAIN
THE VET WOULD SAY
GIVE HIM THIS TABLET
A COUPLE OF TIMES A DAY
LETHARGIC AND WEAK
BACK TO THE VET WE MUST GO
X-RAYS AND SURGERY BAD NEWS WE'RE TOLD

WE MUST SAY GOOD-BYE
TO OUR DEAR FRIEND
THE ANGELS IN HEAVEN
WILL NOW BE YOUR KIN

GOOD LUCK WITH SOCCER
HIDE AND SEEK TOO
EVEN THE ANGELS IN HEAVEN
ARE NO MATCH FOR YOU

WE CALLED HIM GILLIGAN

I DO

DO YOU TAKE THIS MAN? I DO

I DON'T LIKE BLUE SOCKS WITH BROWN SHOES
I DON'T LIKE THAT SHIRT ON YOU
I DON'T THINK YOU HAVE A CLUE

DO YOU TAKE THIS MAN? I DO

I DON'T LIKE THE WAY YOU COMB YOUR HAIR
DO WE ALWAYS HAVE TO GO THERE?
WHY CAN'T I CHOOSE?

DO YOU TAKE THIS MAN? I DO

I DON'T LIKE THE WAY YOU SPEND OUR MONEY
I DON'T LIKE THE JOKES YOU TELL
THEY'RE NOT FUNNY
YOU GIVE ME THE BLUES

DO YOU TAKE THIS MAN? I DO

I DON'T LIKE YOUR MACHO ATTITUDE
WHO DECIDED YOU OWN THE REMOTE HOW RUDE
DON'T THINK SO MUCH BE MORE FEELING
LOGIC LOGIC HOW AM I DEALING
I DON'T GET CUDDLING TIME WITH YOU

DO YOU TAKE THIS MAN? I DO

DO YOU TAKE THIS WOMAN? I DO

I DON'T LIKE YOUR COOKING
MY MOM DOES IT BETTER
SALT PEPPER GARLIC
AMOUNTS DON'T SEEM TO MATTER
AND YOU CALL THIS FOOD?

DO YOU TAKE THIS WOMAN? I DO

I DON'T LIKE YOUR TRIPS TO THE MALL
GONE ALL DAY WITHOUT A CALL
YOUR CLOSET IS PACKED FROM CEILING TO FLOOR
I CAN'T TAKE THIS ANYMORE
WHEN IT COMES TO MONEY YOU LIGHT MY FUSE

DO YOU TAKE THIS WOMAN? I DO

I DON'T LIKE THE WEIGHT YOU'VE GAINED
CAN'T YOU LOOK MORE LIKE WHAT'S HER NAME?
THEN MAYBE I CAN BE TRUE

DO YOU TAKE THIS WOMAN? I DO

I DON'T LIKE YOUR EMOTIONAL CRIES
TOUGHEN UP BE LIKE ONE OF THE GUYS
THE HIGHS THE LOWS WHAT'S WRONG WITH YOU?

DO YOU TAKE THIS WOMAN? I DO

RICHER POORER BETTER OR WORSE
IT DOESN'T MATTER WHO SAID IT FIRST
WHEN THE DON'TS REPLACE THE DOS IN LIFE
SPOKEN BY A HUSBAND OR WIFE
JUST REMEMBER TO WHO YOU SAID I DO

GIRL, SAY IT AIN'T SO

I'M 20-SOMETHING
YOUNG ATTRACTIVE FLYING THE SKIES
SMOKING WHAT I WANT TO SMOKE
NOT MUCH CONCERNED WITH THE WHYS

OFF TO THE ISLANDS MAN JUST THE GIRLS AND I
NOT A CARE IN THE WORLD
NO REASON TO CRY

GIRL, SAY IT AIN'T SO
INFERTILITY INFIDELITY INSECURITY NOT A RED CENT
IYANLA IS RIGHT I'M LIVING IN THE BASEMENT

I'M 30-SOMETHING
BUT STILL RATHER FINE
THINKING ABOUT THAT MAN OF MINE
A WALK DOWN THE AISLE YOU MAY KISS THE BRIDE
OFF TO A HONEYMOON SIDE BY SIDE

NIGHT AFTER NIGHT MUCH LOVE TO SHARE
WHAT FAT YOU SEE THERE'S A BABY IN THERE

GIRL, SAY IT AIN'T SO
LOVE IS BLIND? NOT THIS KIND
OF THE SAME YOKE? I'M LOSING MY MIND
I'M CONFUSED NOT SURE WHAT TO DO
IYANLA FROM THIS FIRST FLOOR I WANT TO MOVE

I'M 40-SOMETHING
OH THAT GRAY HAIR HOW IT SHOWS
DO I? DON'T I? ONLY MY HAIRDRESSER KNOWS
AND THAT BULGE AROUND MY WAIST? DIET EXERCISE
AND THOSE HIPS STILL SEEM OUT OF PLACE

GIRL, SAY IT AIN'T SO
DISEASE DIVORCE MENOPAUSE AND MORE
TEENAGERS HUSBANDS HOT FLASHES GALORE
CHEATING LYING GIRL HE'S GONE
THERAPY PROZAC CAN I HOLD ON

I THINK I KNOW I KNOW I KNOW
IN WHOM I PUT MY TRUST
GOD AND ME WHAT A TEAM
NOTHING CAN BEAT US
OH HOW IT HIT ME DEEP IN MY CORE
IYANLA I'VE MADE IT I'M ON THE SECOND FLOOR

I'M 50 NOW
THEY SAY I'M OVER THE HILL
DOESN'T MUCH BOTHER ME
SMART ENOUGH TO TRUST HIS WILL

OH I'M SLOWER FOR SURE
CAN'T REMEMBER MY NAME
CLIMBING THE STAIRS
BRINGS ON ARTHRITIC PAIN

GIRL, SAY IT AIN'T SO
LOSS OF PARENTS LOVED ONES AND FRIENDS
OH THE 50's HOW THEY BEGIN
BUT I'M SMARTER WISER AND KNOW MORE ABOUT ME
I COUNT MY BLESSINGS AND PUT MY TRUST IN THEE

GIRL, SAY IT AIN'T SO
NO TUNNEL VISION FOR ME
I'VE OPENED MY EYES THE WORLD I SEE
I LIVE ON THE SECOND FLOOR MAKE VISITS TO THE THIRD
NO BASEMENT NO FIRST FLOOR FOR THIS 50-YEAR-OLD GIRL

GIRLFRIEND

IS SHE A COLOR A CLASS A STYLE
OR IS THE TITLE EARNED ONLY AFTER A WHILE?

IS SHE COMMITTED LOYAL TRUSTWORTHY AND KIND
OR LIKE A NEEDLE IN A HAYSTACK – HARD TO FIND?

DID WE GROW UP TOGETHER OR DID WE MEET YESTERDAY?
WHAT'S WITH THIS GIRLFRIEND THING ANYWAY?

IS SHE MOTHER SISTER AUNTIE OR CUZ
CAN SHE BE ANY ONE OF US?

AN EXCLUSIVE GROUP IT SEEMS AT TIMES
HUDDLING TOGETHER WITH A LOVE THAT BINDS

IS SHE SOMEONE WHO KNOWS OUR UPS AND DOWNS
ENCOURAGING US WITH THOSE LAST TEN POUNDS?

AND SOMEONE WHO'S THERE FROM BEGINNING TO END
OUR BIGGEST FAN WHETHER WE LOSE OR WIN?

DO WE LOVE HER RESPECT HER KEEP HER CLOSE AT HEART
PROTECT HER DEFEND HER AS WE OUGHT?

IS THE MEANING ALWAYS WHAT WE INTEND
WHEN WE SO OFTEN SAY, HEY GIRLFRIEND?

SO WHY DO WE USE THIS WORD SO MUCH
CASUALLY SINCERELY ARE WE OUT OF TOUCH?

WE'LL KNOW IN OUR HEARTS WHEN THE NEED IS GREAT
A REAL GIRLFRIEND WON'T BE LATE

THE DANCE

I NOTICED HIM WITH JUST A GLANCE
HOPING HE WOULD ASK ME TO DANCE
HE WALKS TOWARDS ME
HIS BODY BEGINS TO GLIDE
MY HEART IS POUNDING
I'M TREMBLING INSIDE

HIS ARM EXTENDED
LIKE A STRONG STEEL BEAM
HIS HAND SOFT AS COTTON
AT LEAST IT SEEMED

I STAND AND NOD YES
HE LEADS THE WAY
DEAR GOD DON'T LET ME FAINT
I PRAY

HIS ARMS AROUND MY BODY
LIKE THE MOON CIRCLES THE EARTH
I'M GLOWING ALL OVER
AS IF THIS DANCE IS MY FIRST

ON HIS CHEST I SLOWLY REST MY HEAD
A CONVERSATION HAPPENING
WITH NOTHING SAID
I HEAR HIS HEART BEAT IN HARMONY WITH MINE
SERENADING US TO
ANOTHER PLACE AND TIME

THE MUSIC ENDS AND WE MUST PART
BUT NOT THE DANCE WITHIN OUR HEARTS

HE LOVES ME, HE LOVES ME NOT

TODAY HE LOVES ME
TOMORROW HE LOVES ME NOT
IT'S HARD TO TELL
JUST WHAT IT IS I'VE GOT

IT WAS CALLED PUPPY LOVE
WHEN I WAS A TEEN
THE KIND OF LOVE
FOUND ONLY IN A DREAM

EYES CLOSED PLUCKING PETALS
FROM A DAISY
HOPING THE LAST PLUCK
MEANS HE LOVES ME LIKE CRAZY

TEEN YEARS ARE GONE
I WANT LOVE TO LAST
NOT JUST COME AND GO IN A FLASH

UNCONDITIONAL MATURE LOVE
IS HOW IT'S DEFINED
SWEET AND HONEST FORGIVING
AND KIND
IN SICKNESS AND HEALTH GOOD TIMES
AND BAD
NO DAISY PREDICTIONS NO SHORT
TERM FAD

TODAY HE LOVES ME
TOMORROW HE LOVES ME NOT
I FINALLY KNOW WHAT IT IS I'VE GOT

NOW THAT MY FIRST LOVE IS MY LOVE FOR ME
THE LOVE HE GIVES IS PLAIN TO SEE

OPPOSITES

OPPOSITES ATTRACT
SO THEY SAY
BUT IS YOUR OPPOSITE
HERE TO STAY?

SHE LIKES WHITE MEAT
HE LIKES DARK
HE LIKES A 5K RUN
SHE LIKES A STROLL IN THE PARK

HE LIKES ESPN
SHE'S A DISNEY FAN
HE LIKES LENO
SHE LIKES LETTERMAN

HE DRINKS BEER
SHE DRINKS CHAMPAGNE
HE LIKES SPORTING EVENTS
SHE THINKS THEY'RE ALL THE SAME

HE LIKES LOVE-MAKING LATE AT NIGHT
WITH THE LIGHTS ON
SHE LIKES IT WITH THE SUNLIGHT
AT EARLY DAWN

HE LIKES A QUICK SHOWER
SHE LIKES A SOAK IN THE TUB
HE WANTS TO PLAY FOOTIES IN BED
SHE WANTS A FOOT RUB

SO WHAT IF HE LIKES ONE THING
AND SHE LIKES ANOTHER
INCREDIBLY
THESE TWO OPPOSITES
LIKE EACH OTHER

WE JUST DON'T ANYMORE

WE TALK
BUT WE DON'T COMMUNICATE
WE SMILE
BUT WE DON'T LAUGH
UNTIL OUR BELLIES ACHE

WE SLEEP TOGETHER
BUT WE DON'T TOUCH
WE LOOK INTO EACH OTHERS EYES
AND NOT SEE MUCH

WE WATCH TV
BUT ON SEPARATE FLOORS
THERE'S NO OURS
JUST MINE AND YOURS

WE NOW WALK
WHERE WE USED TO DANCE
A HUG OCCASIONALLY
A KISS BY CHANCE

IT SEEMED TO HAPPEN
RIGHT BEFORE OUR EYES
NEVER TOGETHER
NOT WILLING TO COMPROMISE

IN LOVE AND VOWING TO ADORE
SUDDENLY
WE JUST DON'T ANYMORE

YOUR SCENT

WHEREVER I AM
IT FOLLOWS ME IT SEEMS
WRAPPED AROUND MY SENSES
EVEN IN MY DREAMS

YOUR SCENT IS YOURS AND YOURS ALONE
ONE I KNOW NOT POSSIBLE TO CLONE

IN THE MIDST OF THE DAY
IT COMES FLOATING BY
WITH AN AROMA DESTINED TO SATISFY

IT CAN'T BE BOTTLED PACKAGED OR SOLD
ONE OF A KIND MORE PRECIOUS THAN GOLD

THE "N" WORD

I SAW A MOVIE THE OTHER NIGHT
WATCHED BEAUTIFUL MEN AND WOMEN
ACTING WITH ALL THEIR MIGHT
OSCAR PERFORMANCES I WOULD SAY
WORTH THE SEVEN-FIFTY I HAD TO PAY

WHEN OUT OF NOWHERE THE "N" WORD
WAS USED
OVER AND OVER AGAIN
AND I WAS NOT AMUSED

LAUGHTER ECHOING FROM AISLE TO AISLE
IS THIS WHAT SPIKE AND OTHERS WANT ON FILE?

IN THE PARK ON THE STREET
I HEAR IT ALL THE TIME
WHEN ARE WE GOING TO GET IT?
AFRICAN AMERICANS AND THE "N" WORD
ARE NOT OF THE SAME VINE

LET OTHERS CALL US THE "N" WORD
AND WE'RE READY TO KILL
BUT CALL EACH OTHER IT
AS IF IT'S REAL

THERE'S NOTHING HIP
NO BOND TAKING PLACE
CALLING OURSELVES THE "N" WORD
IS A TRUE DISGRACE

OUR ANCESTORS FOUGHT AND DIED
BEING CALLED THE "N" WORD
AND IT'S WHAT SOME OF US CALL OURSELVES
HOW ABSURD

SO WHEN WE'RE CALLED IT
AND BEFORE WE USE IT
THINK ABOUT IT'S HISTORY
THE "N" WORD MUST NOT BE
A PART OF OUR VOCABULARY

THE WEDDING BAND

IT'S PLACED UPON THE FINGER
AS WE SAY I DO
A SYMBOL OF LOVE
BETWEEN BRIDE AND GROOM

SOMETIMES PLATINUM
SOMETIMES GOLD
SOMETIMES IT'S GRANDMA'S
OR HER GRANDMA'S
WE'RE TOLD

PERCHED BEHIND THE ENGAGEMENT RING
AS IF TO PROTECT AND SHIELD
THE WEDDING BAND THE CIRCLE
THAT BINDS AND SEALS

ESPECIALLY ON MOTHER'S DAY

WE MISS YOU MOTHER MORE AND MORE EACH DAY
WITH A VOID IN OUR HEARTS
ESPECIALLY ON MOTHER'S DAY

WE REMEMBER YOU SAYING
YOUR EYES FILLED WITH TEARS
"IT'S MOTHER'S DAY,
I WISH MY MOTHER WAS HERE"

YOU TOLD US THE PAIN WOULD NEVER GO AWAY
YOUR PAIN OF LOSING GRANDMA
WAS APPARENT THAT DAY

YOU SAID "MOTHERS ARE ONLY LOANED TO THEIR KIDS
THIS YOU HAVE TO BELIEVE
GOD WILL DECIDE
WHEN IT'S TIME FOR ME TO LEAVE"

"YES, I MISS YOUR GRANDMOTHER
AFTER MANY YEARS STILL
BUT WE MUST ALWAYS
TRUST IN GOD'S HOLY WILL"

WELL MOTHER, WE'RE TRYING EACH AND EVERY DAY
BUT THE PAIN GETS UNBEARABLE
ESPECIALLY ON MOTHER'S DAY

HAPPY BIRTHDAY, CLOT

WE'VE BEEN TOGETHER SINCE THE WOMB
STRETCHING KICKING NOT MUCH ROOM

THE OLDEST I'M CALLED BUT WHO HAD A CLUE
TWO FIVE POUNDERS NAILLESS HAIRLESS
WAS IT ME OR YOU?

THEY CALLED US THE TWINS FROM THE VERY START
BUT WHAT THEY DIDN'T KNOW
WE'RE SIAMESE TWINS
JOINED AT THE HEART

IT SEEMS WE'VE BEEN INSEPARABLE
SINCE THAT VERY DAY
NOT JUST AS SISTERS
BUT CLOSE IN EVERY WAY

OH WE'VE HAD OUR DISAGREEMENTS FOR SURE
EVERY NOW AND THEN
BUT OUR LOVE FOR ONE ANOTHER
AND THAT TWIN THING WOULD ALWAYS WIN

THEN THAT LITTLE BROTHER WAS BORN
YOU WERE SO JEALOUS YOU BROKE OUT IN HIVES
AND NOW WHAT WOULD WE DO
IF HE WAS NOT PART OF OUR LIVES?

SOMETIMES I LOOK AT YOU
AND WONDER WHAT COULD HAVE BEEN
WE MADE ALL A's AND B's IN SCHOOL
BUT IT WASN'T ENOUGH BACK THEN

GROWING UP IN THE HILLS OF VIRGINIA
WASN'T A PIECE OF CAKE
BUT LOOKING BACK WE KNOW
THAT GOD MAKES NO MISTAKES

WE HAVE NO REGRETS MOTHER TAUGHT US WELL
BE THANKFUL TO GOD FOR WHAT YOU HAVE
AND YOU WILL LIVE TO TELL

THROUGH OUR MARRIAGES
WE ONLY HAD ONE KID SOMEHOW
IN SPITE OF THE BUT MOMMY'S
BUT AUNT CLAUDINE'S
SHE'S MADE US VERY PROUD

NOW WE FIND OURSELVES AT 50
GIRL CAN YOU BELIEVE IT'S TRUE
IT SEEMS LIKE YESTERDAY
WE WERE MAKING MUD PIES
ME AND YOU

WE'VE CRIED AND CRIED OVER THE LOSS OF MOTHER
WE'VE LAUGHED AND LAUGHED AT ONE ANOTHER
I'VE BEEN YOUR THERAPIST AND YOU'VE BEEN MINE
THANKS TO OUR CELL PHONES
WE TALK ALMOST ANY TIME

WE EXERCISE AND TAKE OUR VITAMINS
LIKE THEY SAY WE SHOULD DO IT
AND WE STILL WOULD NIP OR TUCK A COUPLE OF THINGS
IF ONLY WE COULD AFFORD IT

I THINK THEY CALL THIS OVER THE HILL
BUT LIFE IS IN BETTER VIEW
I FEEL VERY BLESSED TODAY, CLOT
TO EXPERIENCE 50 WITH YOU

WE'VE NEVER NEEDED A LOT OF FRIENDS
EVEN THOUGH WE HAVE A BUNCH
WHEN THEIR LIVES BECOME TOO BUSY
FOR YOU OR ME
WE JUST GO HAVE LUNCH

WE'VE TALKED FOR YEARS
ABOUT REACHING THIS AGE
AND WHERE WE'D LIKE TO BE
I'M PROUD TO SAY EMOTIONALLY,
PHYSICALLY, AND SPIRITUALLY
WE'VE BEEN SET FREE

SO TODAY I SAY HAPPY BIRTHDAY
TO MY TWIN, MY FRIEND, MY CONFIDANT
I LOVE SHARING MY LIFE WITH YOU
WHAT MORE COULD I WANT

I LOVE YOU,
CLAUDINE

I WISH MY MOMMY WAS HERE

I HEAR THEM PRAY
NOW I LAY ME DOWN TO SLEEP
DEAR GOD
PLEASE LET MOMMY COME HOME TO ME

TWO PRECIOUS FACES MOIST WITH TEARS
CRYING OUT
I WISH MY MOMMY WAS HERE

OH SWEETHEARTS, I GENTLY SAY
GOD HEARS YOUR CRY
MOMMY WILL BE HOME SOON
TO WIPE YOUR WEARY EYES

I KNOW IT'S BEEN TOO LONG
FOR YOU TO UNDERSTAND
BUT LITTLE ONES
IT'S GOD
WHO'S ALWAYS IN COMMAND

IT WON'T BE EASY
BUT WE MUST WAIT AND PRAY
MOMMY WILL BE HOME
YOU'LL SEE
AND HOME IS WHERE SHE'LL STAY

HOMELESS

I SIT AND STARE DAY AFTER DAY
TRYING TO FIGURE OUT
HOW MY LIFE ENDED UP THIS WAY

I LIVE ON THE STREET
I HAVE FOR SOME TIME
IT'S NOT THAT BAD THOUGH
WELL, MAYBE THE CRIME

I DON'T DO DRUGS, I'M NOT AN ALCOHOLIC
I'M NOT CRAZY
HAD A JOB FOR MANY YEARS
YOU SEE, I'M NOT EVEN LAZY

HOME IS 5TH STREET TODAY
THE HAND-OUTS ARE GOOD
NOT LIKE ON MAIN STREET
WHERE THEY'D WALK ON ME
IF THEY COULD

THE TOSS OF A COIN
A WORN DOLLAR BILL
YOU CAN'T IMAGINE
THE HUMILITY I FEEL

BUT HOME IS WHERE THE HEART IS
I'VE HEARD THEM SAY
SO JUST REMEMBER
WHEN YOU WALK MY WAY

I'M HOMELESS NOT HUMANLESS
I'M HOMELESS NOT USELESS
I'M HOMELESS IT'S NOT CONTAGIOUS
I'M HOMELESS AND I'M COURAGEOUS

FOREVER CAME EARLY

HOW CAN IT BE HERE
'TIL DEATH DO WE PART
IS WHAT FOREVER MEANT
IT SEEMED TO SNEAK UP ON US
WITHOUT THE SLIGHTEST HINT

YET I STILL LOVE YOU
AND YOU LOVE ME
WAS IT THE LITTLE THINGS
OR THE BIG ONES
THAT SET FOREVER FREE

WHAT ABOUT THE VOWS WE MADE
REMEMBER WE SAID I DO
OR THE FOREVER PROMISES
YOU MADE TO ME
AND I MADE TO YOU

FOREVER HAS COME EARLY
BRINGING SUSPICION AND DISTRUST
FOREVER HAS COME EARLY
A SAD MOMENT FOR US

IN LOVE AND COMMITTED
WE SAY NEVER SAY NEVER
IN DOUBT AND BROKEN-HEARTED
WE SAY NEVER SAY FOREVER

I'M OUT OF HERE

I'M OUT OF HERE I CRY
AS I QUICKLY PACK MY THINGS
I'M OUT OF HERE I CRY
REMOVING MY WEDDING RINGS

I'M OUT OF HERE I CRY
AS I SLAM THE DOOR BEHIND ME
I'M OUT OF HERE I CRY
WHAT WILL BE WILL BE

I'M OUT OF THERE I CRY
AS I HASTILY DEPART
I'M OUT OF THERE I CRY
BUT I FORGOT TO PACK MY HEART

ON NIGHTS LIKE THIS

NO MATTER WHAT ANYONE SAYS
TIME DOES NOT PULL YOU THROUGH
BECAUSE THERE ARE NIGHTS
WHEN WE STILL CRY OUT FOR YOU

SOMETIMES IT SWALLOWS US
THIS EMPTY SPACE WE FEEL INSIDE
WE THINK OF HOW STRONG YOU WERE
AND IT HELPS US TO GET BY

ON NIGHTS LIKE THIS
THERE'S THE ANGER
THAT BLOCKS OUT THE LIGHT
ON NIGHTS LIKE THIS
THERE'S THE DOUBT
THAT HOLDS US CAPTIVE
NIGHT AFTER NIGHT

ON NIGHTS LIKE THIS
WE KNOW YOU'RE IN A BETTER PLACE
ON NIGHTS LIKE THIS
WE PRAY
WE'LL BE WITH YOU AGAIN SOMEDAY

STAY IN CONTROL

WHAT'S UP WITH THAT QUICK TO ANGER STYLE
LIFE'S TOO SHORT FOR THAT MUCH STRESS
CHILL OUT FOR A WHILE

NOTHING AND NO ONE IS WORTH ONE'S HEALTH
NOT WINNING NOT LOSING NOT EVEN GREAT WEALTH

YES, ANGER IS A FEELING AND NEEDS TO BE EXPRESSED
HOW FAR WE GO IN EXPRESSING IT
IS THE ULTIMATE TEST

SO BE COOL BE CALM
LET COMPROMISE BE YOUR GOAL
DON'T LET ANGER BE THE RULER
YOU STAY IN CONTROL

MY CHILD THAT NEVER WAS

I PLAYED WITH DOLLS AS EARLY AS I CAN RECALL
DRESSING THEM FOR SCHOOL PARTIES AND ALL

GIVING EACH ONE A NAME
PRETENDING WAS SO SWELL
BEING A MOMMY SOMEDAY
WOULD BE WONDERFUL
I COULD JUST TELL

BUT IT NEVER HAPPENED
GOD HAD OTHER PLANS FOR ME
GODMOTHER AND AUNTIE

I STILL LONG FOR MY CHILD THAT NEVER WAS
HAVE NO ANSWERS WHY
BUT WHO DOES?

WOULD SHE BE BRIGHT?
WOULD HER SPIRIT BE LIKE MINE?
OR LIKE HER GRANDMOTHER'S –
SASSY MOST OF THE TIME?

WOULD SHE BE A LOVER OF LIFE
LIKE I WOULD HAVE HOPED?
WOULD LIFE HAVE TREATED HER UNJUSTLY?
WOULD SHE HAVE COPED?

A MYSTERY TO ME
THIS UNBORN CHILD OF MINE
MY CHILD THAT NEVER WAS
COMFORTS ME FROM TIME TO TIME

SHE WILL ALWAYS BE INSIDE OF ME
NO LABOR PAINS NO BIRTH
SHE WILL LIVE IN MY HEART AND SOUL
JUST NOT ON THIS HERE EARTH

THAT UNRELENTING STARE

AT FIRST I THOUGHT IT WAS AN INNOCENT
LINGERING GLANCE
BUT AFTER A FEW MOMENTS
I KNEW THERE WAS NO CHANCE

THIS WAS A STARE
AN UNRELENTING ONE AT THAT
FROM A STRANGER NO DOUBT
SOMEONE I HAD NOT MET

WITHOUT LOOKING
I KNOW IT'S STILL THERE
I FEEL IT PENETRATE MY BODY
THAT UNRELENTING STARE

SO I SPEAK
HOPING THAT AN END WOULD SOON BE NEAR
I GET A NOD
AND IT BECOMES QUITE CLEAR

THERE MUST BE A RUN IN MY HOSE
OR AN UNIDENTIFIABLE OBJECT ON MY NOSE
SOMETHING IS OUT OF SORTS SOMEWHERE
IT WON'T GIVE UP
THAT UNRELENTING STARE

TO END THIS INTRUSION
I WALK AWAY IN HASTE
APPARENTLY WHAT I'M FEELING
ISN'T SHOWING ON MY FACE

SO DON'T BE SURPRISED
SOMEDAY SOMEWHERE
WHEN YOU'RE CONFRONTED BY
THAT UNRELENTING STARE

THIS PAIN THIS HEARTACHE

NOT SURE IF I'LL MAKE IT THROUGH ANOTHER DAY
THIS PAIN THIS HEARTACHE
PLEASE GO AWAY

I TRIED LONG WALKS
MEDITATING TOO
COLD SHOWERS HOT SHOWERS
NOTHING WILL DO

THIS PAIN THIS HEARTACHE
IS MAKING ME BLUE
THIS PAIN THIS HEARTACHE
OVER LOSING YOU

WILL IT EVER DISSIPATE?
JUST EASE UP SOME
THIS PAIN THIS HEARTACHE
I PRAY RELIEF WILL COME

WILL IT TAKE ANOTHER DAY MONTH OR YEAR?
IT MAY BE WITH ME FOREVER
THIS IS MY FEAR

TIME HEALS ALL WOUNDS
OPTIMISTS SAY
THEY DIDN'T LOVE YOU DEEPLY
IN A SPECIAL WAY

BUT IF IT'S TRUE
INDEED IT MAY BE
I NEED TIME'S HEALING POWER
TO RESCUE ME

THIS PAIN THIS HEARTACHE
A QUICK FIX I WISH I KNEW
THIS PAIN THIS HEARTACHE
OVER LOSING YOU

LET'S SNEAK AWAY

LET'S SNEAK AWAY
FOR AN HOUR OR TWO
A BASKET IN HAND
FULL OF LOVE FOR ME AND YOU

LET'S SNEAK AWAY
WE NEED IT
YOU SEE
THE BUSY WORLD IS STEALING "US"
FROM YOU AND ME

LET'S SNEAK AWAY
FOR AN HOUR OR TWO
THEN BACK TO THE BUSY WORLD
AT PEACE AND RENEWED

YOUR WORDS

YOUR WORDS CUT INTO MY SOUL
LIKE THE BLADE OF A KNIFE

YOUR WORDS SLICE THE SPIRIT
RIGHT OUT OF MY LIFE

YOUR WORDS HAVE DRIVEN ME
EMOTIONALLY AWAY

YOU'LL START TO SPEAK
AND I'LL BE GONE SOMEDAY

LOST POWER

I LOST MY POWER IN THE MIDST OF OUR MESS
NO STRENGTH TO FIGHT BACK
I MUST CONFESS

I FELT HELPLESS OUT OF CONTROL
EMPTY INSIDE
FOUND A HOLE WITH A COVER
IN WHICH TO HIDE

SLEEPLESSNESS AND ANXIETY
LAY WITH ME EACH NIGHT
DEPRESSION AND SADNESS
WERE MY MORNING LIGHT

THEN I BEGAN TO PRAY
WITH A SOLID LOOK INTO MY SOUL
AND SLOWLY REMOVED THE COVER
FROM THAT DARK DEEP HOLE

GLIMPSES OF POWER
BEGAN TO SHINE THROUGH
ENORMOUS STRENGTH
THAT WAS LONG OVER DUE

MY POWER WAS NEVER LOST
OR TAKEN AWAY
JUST MISPLACED
IN A STRANGE SORT OF WAY

NO ONE TAKES YOUR POWER AWAY
IT'S A CHOICE TO LET IT GO
IT'S YOURS TO SELL OR GIVE AWAY
OR KEEP FOREVER STORED

SO DON'T LOOK OUTWARD
FOR POWER THAT IS LOST
LOOK DEEP WITHIN
TO RECLAIM ONE'S LOST POWER
IT'S THE ONLY PLACE TO BEGIN

WILL YOU BE MINE?

IT'S VALENTINE'S DAY AND WE WILL ALL
ASK THAT INFAMOUS QUESTION
WILL YOU BE MINE?
I'VE GIVEN THIS SOME THOUGHT
FROM TIME TO TIME

THERE WILL BE ENGAGEMENTS WEDDINGS
LOVE IN THE AIR
ON VALENTINE'S DAY
IT SEEMS TO BE EVERYWHERE

FLORISTS WILL MAKE LOTS OF MONEY TODAY
THE CANDY MAN IS CERTAINLY HAVING HIS WAY
IT'S OUR EXPRESSION OF LOVE
ON VALENTINE'S DAY

FLOWERS WILL BE SENT FROM COAST TO COAST
FLOWERS ARE NICE
BUT IT'S YOUR UNCONDITIONAL LOVE
THAT I WANT MOST

CANDY IS SWEET AND COMES PACKED IN A HEART
A VALENTINE MESSAGE WITH A LOVING THOUGHT
WILL YOU BE MINE
NO MATTER WHAT STORMS COME
OR AT THE FIRST SIGN OF TROUBLE
UP AND RUN?

WILL YOU BE MINE
WHEN THE BILLS ARE DUE
MONEY IS SHORT
AND THE KIDS HAVE THE FLU?

WILL YOU BE MINE
WHEN THE GOOD
IS NOT SO EASY TO SEE
WILL YOU BE MINE
WHEN I'M NOT AS TIDY AS I COULD BE?

WILL YOU BE MINE
IF I FORGET A SPECIAL DATE
WILL YOU BE MINE
IF I'M TIRED
AND COME HOME LATE?

WILL YOU BE MINE
IF I SAY NOT TONIGHT
AND STILL BE MINE
WHETHER I'M WRONG OR RIGHT?

WILL YOU BE MINE
WHEN I'M HAVING A BAD DAY
FORGIVE ME AND LOVE ME ANYWAY?

NOW LOOK AT YOUR LOVER
AND PONDER THIS THOUGHT

WHEN THE CANDY IS GONE
AND THE FLOWERS HAVE DIED
WILL YOU STILL BE MINE
RIGHT BY MY SIDE?

THE STRANGER IN MY BED

PHYSICALLY I KNOW IT'S YOU
YOU ANSWER WHEN I CALL YOUR NAME
MY LOVER MY FRIEND MY CONFIDANT
BUT SOMEHOW YOU'RE NOT THE SAME

A STRANGER IN MY BED IS WHAT YOU'VE BECOME
YOUR TOUCH ONCE SO SOOTHING
NOW MAKES ME NUMB

THE STRANGER IN MY BED
I'VE LOVED FOR MANY YEARS
THE STRANGER IN MY BED
NOW BRINGS ME TO TEARS

THE STRANGER IN MY BED
I WOULD LIKE TO GET TO KNOW AGAIN
BUT WITH THE STRANGER IN MY BED
JUST WHERE WOULD I BEGIN

I MISSED YOU TODAY

I AWOKE THIS MORNING AND MY THOUGHTS
WERE ABOUT LAST NIGHT
HOW YOU HELD ME IN YOUR ARMS
AND MADE EVERYTHING SEEM RIGHT

THE ALARM BEEPED IN THE SAME OLD WAY
SUMMONING ME TO A BRAND NEW DAY

THE SUNLIGHT'S GLOW CALLED ME BY NAME
I LAID THERE MISSING YOU
ALL THE SAME

I PASSED OUR FAVORITE PICNIC SPOT
AND COULD ALMOST FEEL YOUR TOUCH
NOT SURPRISED THAT I MISSED YOU TODAY
JUST SURPRISED HOW MUCH

I HEARD OUR SONG ON THE RADIO
AND BEGAN TO DANCE OUR DANCE
WANTED YOU TO KNOW I MISSED YOU TODAY
WHILE I HAD THE CHANCE

SO HURRY HOME MY SWEET LOVE
DON'T LINGER ALONG THE WAY
I NEED TO SHOW YOU JUST HOW MUCH
I MISSED YOU TODAY

HANDCUFFED

I WATCHED THEM DRAG HIM ALL ALONG
WONDERING TO WHAT MOTHER HE BELONGED

THE VISIBLE SCARS WERE BLACK AND BLUE
THE INVISIBLE ONES RANG LOUD AND TRUE

HIS LOOK WAS FRIGHTENING IN A SAD SORT OF WAY
WHY WAS HE HANDCUFFED THIS PARTICULAR DAY?

HIS EYES FILLED WITH ANGER HOPELESSNESS AND GRIEF
MOURNING THE DEATH OF LIFE
HANDCUFFED WITH DEFEAT

HANDCUFFED BY LIFE THE DAY HE WAS BORN
A MOTHER A FATHER
A RELATIONSHIP TORN

ON HIS OWN AT THE AGE OF SIX
RELIEVING THE PAIN
WITH THE STREET'S QUICK FIX

MADE GOOD GRADES WHEN HE DID ATTEND SCHOOL
BUT THE FAST STREET LIFE CALLED HIM A FOOL

WHETHER BORN IN POVERTY OR IN GREAT WEALTH
HANDCUFFED IS HANDCUFFED
BY THEM OR LIFE ITSELF

IF ONLY THE HANDCUFFS HAD NOT BEEN IGNORED
THE INVISIBLE ONES THAT CAGED HIM
AND AMPLIFIED HIS ROAR

THE SCARS DEEP WITHIN RIPPED HIS SELF ESTEEM
MASKING WHO HE REALLY IS
DESTROYING HIS LIFE DREAMS

SO NOW WE LABEL HIM "MONSTER"
THE KIND WE LOCK AWAY
HAD WE TAKEN THE TIME TO NOTICE
THE HANDCUFFS MIGHT NOT HAVE STAYED

MY MIND IS WAITING FOR MY HEART

IN MY MIND I KNOW I SHOULD LEAVE
BUT IT'S MY HEART I MUST RETRIEVE

WHY DO I STILL CARE?
MY MIND WANTS TO ASK
MY MIND IS ANGRY WITH THOUGHTS OF THE PAST

MY HEART SAYS ONE LAST CHANCE
CAN'T WE GIVE IN?
MY MIND SAYS NO
THAT PLACE YOU KNOW WE'VE BEEN

WHAT ABOUT FOLLOW YOUR HEART?
REMEMBER WE'RE TOLD
MY MIND REMEMBERS
LOVE BEING CALLOUS AND COLD

CONFUSING THIS TUG OF WAR
BETWEEN MY MIND AND HEART
MY HEART WANTS TO TRY AGAIN
MY MIND WANTS TO DEPART

WITH EACH HEART BEAT
COMES THE SOUNDS OF FORGIVE AND FORGET
THE THOUGHTS ECHOING FROM MY MIND
ARE RUN DON'T LOOK BACK YET

SO UNTIL MY HEART CATCHES UP WITH MY MIND
A TUG OF WAR IS WHAT I WILL FIND

I DIDN'T GET TO SAY GOODBYE

I KNEW YOU WERE ILL
VERY ILL IN FACT
BUT I WAS TOLD
YOU'LL HAVE TIME TO GET BACK

DOCTORS GIVE US SIX MONTHS
THREE MONTHS ONE MONTH
TO LIVE
I SHOULD HAVE KNOWN
TIME ON EARTH
IS ONLY GOD'S TO GIVE

BUT I BELIEVED THEM
AND REGRETTABLY
I WASN'T THERE
WHETHER YOUR PLAN OR GOD'S PLAN
IT DOESN'T SEEM QUITE FAIR

I KNOW YOU LOVED ME
MAYBE THAT WAS THE KEY
TAKING YOUR LAST BREATH
WAS NOT SOMETHING
YOU WANTED ME TO SEE

WATCHING YOU GO
WOULD HAVE BEEN A BURDEN TO BEAR
STILL I WANTED AND NEEDED
TO BE THERE

I KNOW YOU KNEW I LOVED YOU
THAT'S NOT THE REASON WHY
JUST HOW DO I HAVE CLOSURE
WITHOUT HAVING SAID GOODBYE

THE DAMAGE RUNS TOO DEEP

REPAIRABLE WE HAVE HOPED
FOR UNDERSTANDING WE HAVE PRAYED
OUR MARRIAGE OUR PRIORITY
UNTIL YOU STRAYED

OUR LOVE WAS STRONG
WE COULD CONQUER ALL
THEN YOU FAILED TO TALK TO ME
THE BEGINNING OF OUR FALL

YOU HAVE WORKED HARD
AND SO HAVE I
WHATEVER THE THERAPIST SAID MIGHT WORK
WE HAVE TRIED

FORGIVENESS A POSSIBILITY
WITH THE PATIENCE OF TIME
FORGETTING NOT PROBABLE
YOUR STRAYING ENGULFS MY MIND

WE WITNESS OUR LOVE
SHATTERING BEYOND REPAIR
OUR EYES FILLED WITH TEARS
WE WEEP IN DESPAIR

OUR MARRIAGE IS OVER
OUR VOWS WE COULD NOT KEEP
THE SCARS THE HEARTBREAK
THE DAMAGE RUNS TOO DEEP

ON MY OWN

A SENSE OF FREEDOM
ON MY OWN

A SENSE OF LIFE
ON MY OWN

A SENSE OF COMFORT
ON MY OWN

A SENSE OF WELL BEING
ON MY OWN

A SENSE OF COURAGE
ON MY OWN

A SENSE OF LAUGHTER
ON MY OWN

A SENSE OF CONTROL
ON MY OWN

A SENSE OF ME
ON MY OWN